D0772717

MAN-MADE DISASTERS
HINDENBURG

by Jenny Fretland VanVoorst

pogo

Ideas for Parents and Teachers

Pogo Books let children practice reading informational text while introducing them to nonfiction features such as headings, labels, sidebars, maps, and diagrams, as well as a table of contents, glossary, and index.

Carefully leveled text with a strong photo match offers early fluent readers the support they need to succeed.

Before Reading

• "Walk" through the book and point out the various nonfiction features. Ask the student what purpose each feature serves.

• Look at the glossary together. Read and discuss the words.

Read the Book

• Have the child read the book independently.

• Invite him or her to list questions that arise from reading.

After Reading

• Discuss the child's questions. Talk about how he or she might find answers to those questions.

• Prompt the child to think more. Ask: Did you know about the *Hindenburg* explosion before reading this book? What more do you want to learn after reading it?

Pogo Books are published by Jump!
5357 Penn Avenue South
Minneapolis, MN 55419
www.jumplibrary.com

Library of Congress Cataloging-in-Publication Data

Names: Fretland VanVoorst, Jenny, 1972- author.
Title: Hindenburg / by Jenny Fretland VanVoorst.
Description: Minneapolis, MN: Jump!, Inc., [2018]
Series: Man-made disasters | Audience: Ages 7-10.
Identifiers: LCCN 2017035679 (print)
LCCN 2017035229 (ebook)
ISBN 9781624967047 (ebook)
ISBN 9781620319208 (hardcover : alk. paper)
ISBN 9781620319215 (pbk.)
Subjects: LCSH: Hindenburg (Airship)—Juvenile literature. | Aircraft accidents—New Jersey—History—20th century—Juvenile literature. Airships—History—Juvenile literature. Airships—Germany—History—Juvenile literature.
Classification: LCC TL659.H5 (print)
LCC TL659.H5 F74 2018 (ebook) | DDC 363.12/4—dc23
LC record available at https://lccn.loc.gov/2017035679

Editor: Kristine Spanier
Book Designer: Michelle Sonnek
Photo Researcher: Michelle Sonnek

Photo Credits: Bettmann/Getty, cover, 18-19; SeM/UIG/Getty, 1; Eye-Stock/Alamy, 3; INTERFOTO/Alamy, 4; World History Archive/Alamy, 5; New York Daily News Archive/Getty, 6-7, 15; Chones/Shutterstock, 8 (foreground); John Frost Newspapers/Alamy, 8 (background); Paul Bradbury/iStock, 9; ullstein bild Dtl./Getty, 10-11; Contraband Collection/Alamy, 12-13 (foreground); Cartarium/Shutterstock, 12-13 (background); Hulton Archive/Getty, 14; Sueddeutsche Zeitung Photo/Alamy, 16-17; Pincasso/Shutterstock, 20-21, AJE/Shutterstock, 23 (foreground); Standard Studio/Shutterstock, 23 (background).

Printed in the United States of America at Corporate Graphics in North Mankato, Minnesota.

TABLE OF CONTENTS

CHAPTER 1
Fire in the Night 4

CHAPTER 2
The Airship Era 8

CHAPTER 3
The Disaster 14

ACTIVITIES & TOOLS
Try This! 22
Glossary 23
Index 24
To Learn More 24

CHAPTER 1

FIRE IN THE NIGHT

The date was May 6, 1937. The sky was dark. The *Hindenburg* dropped its landing lines. It had rained all day, and at 7 P.M. the sun was setting.

Suddenly the air exploded with orange light. Flames filled the night sky. The giant airship was on fire!

People on the ground ran. Passengers jumped out of its windows. It took just over 30 seconds for the entire airship to go up in flames. In that time, 36 people died. With them died the future of airships.

DID YOU KNOW?

Video of the disaster is online. You can also hear the famous audio recording made by a reporter.

CHAPTER 2

THE AIRSHIP ERA

Today we travel across the ocean in airplanes. But in the early 1900s, airships were thought to be the future of overseas travel.

Germany Builds a—
Great New AIR GIANT
80 m.p.h. Zeppelin as Big as a Liner

April 14, 1934—SCOOPS

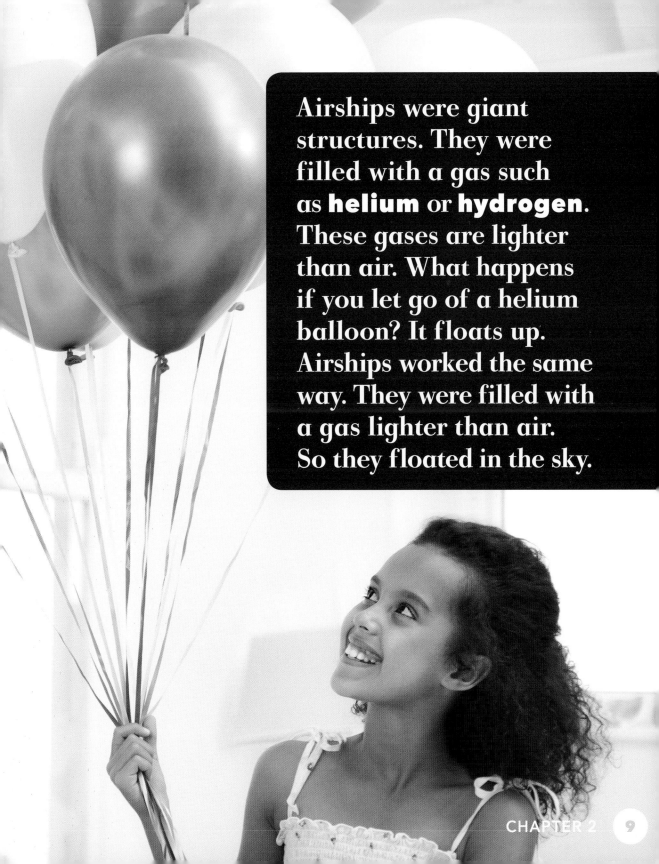

Airships were giant structures. They were filled with a gas such as **helium** or **hydrogen**. These gases are lighter than air. What happens if you let go of a helium balloon? It floats up. Airships worked the same way. They were filled with a gas lighter than air. So they floated in the sky.

Airships mostly held gas. But they had a small area for passengers, **crew**, and **cargo**.

The *Hindenburg* was a huge airship. It could hold more than 100 people.

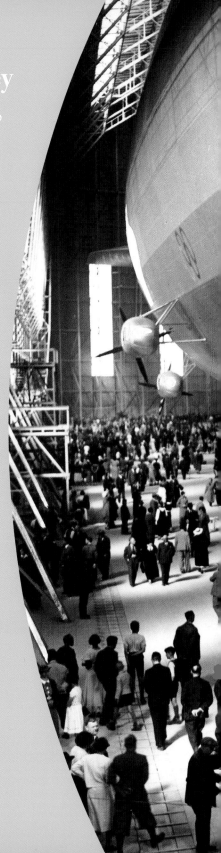

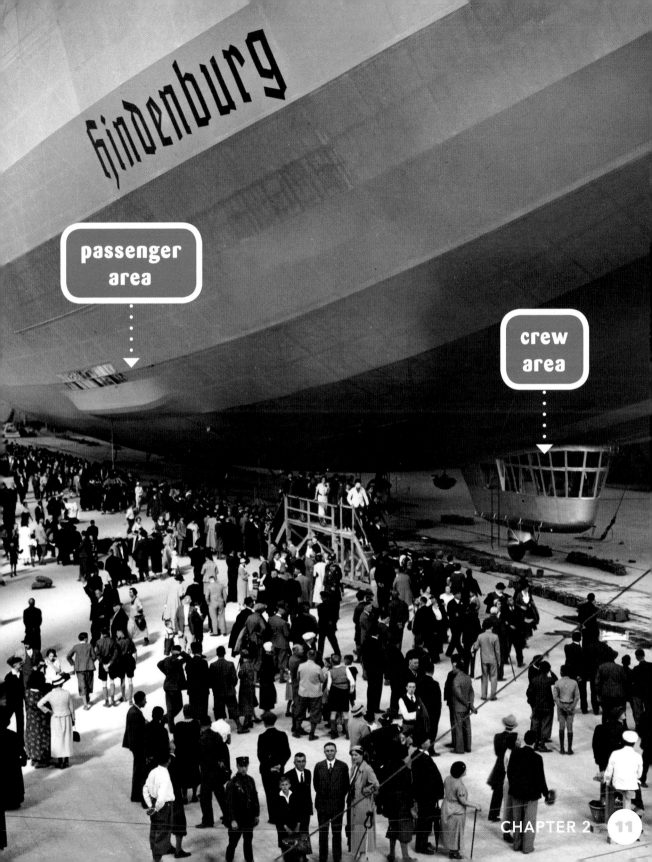

passenger
area

crew
area

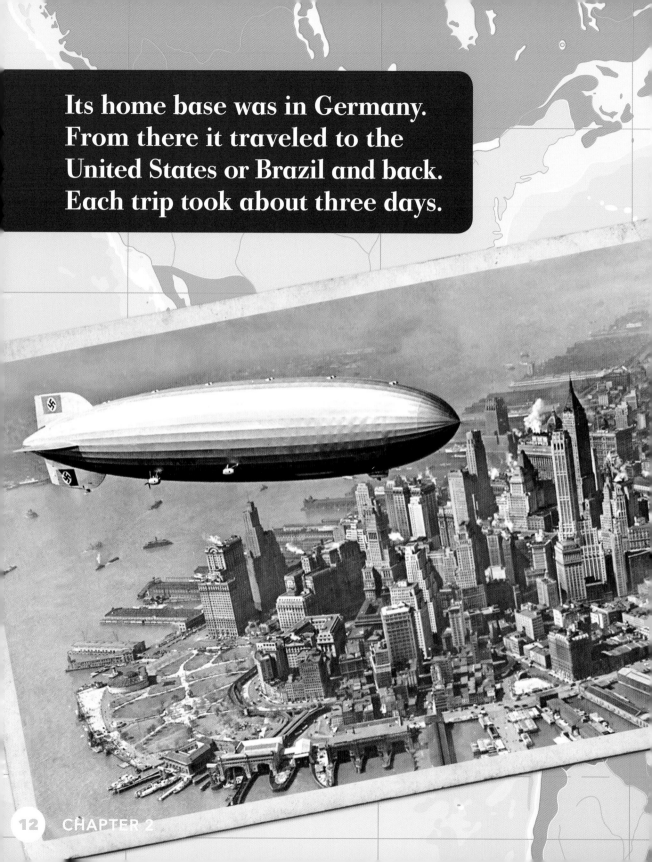

Its home base was in Germany. From there it traveled to the United States or Brazil and back. Each trip took about three days.

TAKE A LOOK!

The *Hindenburg* was three times as long as the airplanes we travel in today.

- **Capacity:** 40-62 crew and 50-72 passengers
- **Length:** 804 feet (245 meters)
- **Diameter:** 135 feet (41 m)
- **Maximum speed:** 84 miles per hour (135 kilometers per hour)
- **Final flight:** Frankfurt, Germany, to Lakehurst, New Jersey, May 3-6, 1937

CHAPTER 3

THE DISASTER

In the spring of 1937, the *Hindenburg* was in its second year of service. It had made 63 flights. None had been eventful.

But this flight was different. As the airship tried to dock, it burst into flames. Why?

docking station

Most scientists believe the following chain of events was the likely cause:

First, a tear in the **hull** let hydrogen escape. This gas is **flammable**.

During the flight, **static electricity** built up on the hull. When the landing ropes hit the ground, it **discharged**.

The electricity lit the hydrogen on fire. It exploded.

DID YOU KNOW?

The *Hindenburg* was built to be filled with helium. Helium is not flammable. But there were laws limiting its sale. The Germans used hydrogen instead.

The lit gas shot flames into the air. The fuel caught fire. Burning fuel fell to the ground. The entire airship was destroyed.

DID YOU KNOW?

The hull material may have been fuel for the fire. Its coating was similar to the fuel used to power rockets!

fuel

The *Hindenburg* disaster happened at the same time airplane travel was beginning to take off. Airplanes were faster than airships. They were also safer. In the end, airplanes prevailed. Airships no longer float in the skies.

ACTIVITIES & TOOLS

AIRSHIP BALLAST

Helium balloons float up and away. So how does an airship, which is similarly filled with a lighter-than-air gas, keep from floating off into the sky? It has tanks filled with regular air. This weight is called ballast. When the airship wants to rise, it releases some of the ballast, making it lighter. When it wants to descend, it opens the tanks to let in air, making it heavier. Let's see how this works on a helium balloon, using pennies for ballast. (Make sure to try this inside so you don't lose your balloon!)

What You Need:
- one helium-filled balloon
- handful of pennies
- tape

❶ Hold the balloon lightly by its string. Tape pennies one by one to the balloon until it stops ascending and simply hangs in the air when you release the string. How many pennies does it take until the balloon simply floats in place?

❷ Now add more pennies to bring the balloon to the floor. How many more pennies does it take?

❸ Now release the pennies one by one until the balloon lifts off and continues to ascend.

GLOSSARY

cargo: Goods being transported.

crew: A group of people working together to operate and staff an aircraft or other vehicle.

discharged: Released.

flammable: Capable of being easily set on fire and burning rapidly.

helium: A nonflammable, colorless gas that is lighter than air.

hull: The frame or body of a boat or airship.

hydrogen: A colorless, odorless, and highly flammable gas.

static electricity: Electricity that consists of charges that build up on the surface of an object, usually as the result of rubbing.

INDEX

airplanes 8, 13, 20

airship 5, 7, 8, 9, 10, 15, 19, 20

Brazil 12

cargo 10

crew 10, 13

disaster 7, 20

discharged 16

dock 15

exploded 5, 16

fire 5, 16, 19

flames 5, 7, 15, 19

flammable 16

flights 13, 14, 15, 16

fuel 19

gas 9, 10, 16, 19

Germany 12, 13

helium 9, 16

hull 16, 19

hydrogen 9, 16

passengers 7, 10, 13

scientists 16

static electricity 16

travel 8, 12, 13, 20

United States 12

TO LEARN MORE

Learning more is as easy as 1, 2, 3.

1) Go to www.factsurfer.com

2) Enter "Hindenburg" into the search box.

3) Click the "Surf" button to see a list of websites.

With factsurfer, finding more information is just a click away.